Kin
&
Queens
OF ENGLAND

Written by Louise Jones
Illustrated by John Dillow

ABOUT THIS BOOK

The story of how each of England's kings and queens came to rule
the kingdom is told in the captivating words and pictures of
Kings and Queens of England.
The major dramatic events of each reign
are featured in the main text.
Additional pictures and captions in the margins of the book
expand the full, rich picture of times past – from the prosperous
reign of Henry VII to the family troubles of Queen Elizabeth II.
The foldout family tree shows the relationships between
different monarchs.

Main illustrations by John Dillow
Portrait illustrations by Jon Jackson

Ladybird books are widely available, but in case of
difficulty may be ordered by post or telephone from:

Ladybird Books – Cash Sales Department
Littlegate Road Paignton Devon TQ3 3BE
Telephone 01803 554761

A catalogue record for this book is available
from the British Library

Published by Ladybird Books Ltd Loughborough Leicestershire UK

© LADYBIRD BOOKS LTD MCMXCVI
LADYBIRD and the device of a Ladybird are trademarks of Ladybird Books Ltd
All rights reserved. No part of this publication may be reproduced,
stored in a retrieval system, or transmitted in any form or by any
means, electronic, mechanical, photocopying, recording or otherwise,
without the prior consent of the copyright owner.

CONTENTS

INTRODUCTION

King Arthur's sword 'Excalibur', from a book entitled **Morte d'Arthur** *(Death of Arthur). It was published in 1485 by William Caxton (below) the first English printer. Printing changed society for ever.*

W Ꝋ ꝇ

The history of England from the Norman Conquest in 1066 was closely linked with the history of France. In battle after battle, French territory passed to and fro between England and France. The worst of this fighting, the Hundred Years War, had ended in 1453, but conflict between the two countries was not over. In England itself, opposing members of the royal family had been fighting for the crown.

Gradually, though, life was becoming more settled and peaceful. The **feudal system**, which had caused such misery, had gone. The **Renaissance** was flowering in 15th-century Europe. Exploration of the globe, foreign trading, and scientific and artistic achievement were increasingly important in English life.

As international travel and trading grew, European rulers and merchant seamen became interested in finding an easier, western route to Asia. They especially wanted to reach the Asian islands of the East Indies, then known as the Spice Islands because of the many precious spices which grew there. John Cabot was an Italian who settled in England in about 1484. In 1497, accompanied by his 18-year old son Sebastian, he sailed in search of the 'Northwest Passage' to Asia, for Henry VII.

They sailed from Bristol. A customs official called Richard Ameryke was instructed by King Henry to pay the Cabots the money they needed. In June the Cabots landed on what they thought to be the China coast. Without realising it, they had discovered America – perhaps named after the customs official Richard Ameryke who had funded the trip. In 1492 Christopher Columbus on behalf of the Spanish King Ferdinand V, had also sailed in search of a western route to Asia and accidentally first found America.

In 9th-century England the early Saxon kings had driven the native Celts from power. Since 1066 English monarchs had been French, or partly so. Now, under the Tudors, England was ruled again by monarchs with Celtic blood.

The development of gunpowder changed the nature of war.

The Cabots' ship, Matthew. On this voyage in 1497 Cabot and his crew found North America, but thought it was Asia.

HENRY VII
1485-1509 (b. 1457)

The impostor Lambert Simnel working as a kitchen boy in Henry's kitchens.

Henry created this court of justice. It was named the Court of the Star Chamber after the stars painted on its ceiling.

Henry Tudor's victory over Richard III at the Battle of Bosworth Field, in 1485, ended thirty years of bitter fighting for the crown between the House of Lancaster and the House of York. This struggle is known as the **Wars of the Roses**.

Henry VII was a Lancastrian. To make sure peace continued, in the year after the Battle of Bosworth Field, he married Elizabeth of York. She was the eldest daughter of the late Edward IV, a Yorkist king. Henry's marriage to Elizabeth united the feuding houses of Lancaster and York, and in this way he became the first king of a new royal house. This new house became known as 'Tudor', from Henry's surname.

The early years of Henry's reign were still troubled by Yorkist claims to the throne. Two claimants

were impostors: the first, Lambert Simnel, had been coached by a group of Yorkists to pretend that he was Edward IV's nephew. The 12-year old Simnel was crowned Edward VI in Dublin in 1487. But in the same year Henry defeated the plotters, and made

Simnel a kitchen-hand. The other impostor, Perkin Warbeck, troubled Henry for much longer. Warbeck was arrested in 1497, but continued his trouble-making even in captivity. He was executed in 1499.

Pembroke Castle (Wales), Henry's birthplace, and his personal standard, the red dragon of Wales. Henry was Welsh on his father's side.

Henry was a strong, learned and thoughtful king, who was fair in lawgiving, and very good at making and keeping money. His long reign brought peace and prosperity after many troubled years. However, he was never much loved by his subjects, for he lacked warmth and charm.

Perkin Warbeck's execution. Warbeck enlisted the support of many foreign rulers for his claim to be Richard, brother of the tragic Edward V (the boy-king who had been imprisoned and had died in the Tower of London).

HENRY VIII
1509-1547 (b. 1491)

With the voyages of the great explorers, the wealth of distant lands could be acquired; in 1524, turkeys were brought from South America.

One of the warships Henry had built in 1511, when he overhauled the Royal Navy. Each ship weighed 1,000 tons.

Henry VII had two sons. Arthur, the elder son, had died young, and so his brother, Henry, became the next king.

Henry VIII was handsome and charming, and was welcomed by the people. He married Arthur's young widow, the Spanish Catherine of Aragon, and seemed destined for a happy reign. But after twenty years he became obsessed with the need for a son and **heir**, and wanted a new wife. The Church did not allow divorce. Henry claimed that his marriage was not valid, because marriage to a brother's widow was not allowed (he had had special permission for his marriage). The

atherine of Aragon

Anne Boleyn

Jane Seymour

Anne of Cleves

Catherine Howard

Catherine Parr

Pope would not agree to a divorce, and so Henry officially denied the Pope's authority and divorced Catherine.

In 1531 Henry broke away from the Roman Catholic Church and declared himself head of a separate English Church. He closed the monasteries in England and took their treasures. Yet he was not sympathetic to Protestants, believing himself a Catholic despite his actions.

Henry married five more times after his divorce from Catherine. Of his six wives only Jane Seymour bore him the son he wanted. She died in childbirth.

Henry was a wilful, powerful man, who changed the course of English history to get what he wanted, and killed those who displeased him.

Henry's pursuit of a son and heir to ensure the continuation of the new Tudor line led him into six marriages. He seemed happy with Edward VI's mother, Jane Seymour, but she died giving birth to Edward. He divorced Anne of Cleves for being too ugly; Catherine Howard lost her head for being unfaithful to him. Edward remained his only son.

EDWARD VI
1547-1553 (b. 1537)

EDWARD VI

Edward was only ten when his father died, so government was in the hands of a group of lords called the Regency Council. Edward's uncle, the Duke of Somerset, bribed other Council members to put him in charge, with the title Lord Protector. Somerset was very ambitious, but also kind and indecisive.

16th-century village life had been disrupted by 'enclosure'. This was the hedging and fencing of land so that the landowners could keep sheep on it. The peasants were angry and worried. In 1549, many rebelled; Robert Kett, a Norfolk man, led 16,000 rebels. Somerset's delay in setting the army on the rebels lost him support from the **aristocracy**, and the ruthless Duke of Northumberland took his place.

Land enclosure riots. Public anger grew throughout the 16th century, as landowners fenced off land that had been in common use. In 1549, rioting erupted countrywide.

Northumberland was ambitious and selfish. The English Protestant Church was established in 1549-52, and Northumberland punished and imprisoned many loyal Catholics. He also married one of his sons to Lady Jane Grey, a sweet-natured and brilliant granddaughter of Henry VIII's younger sister. Edward fell gravely ill with tuberculosis. Northumberland persuaded him to make Lady Jane his heir, claiming that Henry VIII's marriages to Catherine of Aragon, Mary's mother, and Anne Boleyn, Elizabeth's mother, had been **invalid**. Edward died and on 10 July 1553 the unwilling Lady Jane was named queen. Supporters rallied to Edward's half-sister, Princess Mary, and on 19 July 1553 the Regency Council declared her queen instead. Lady Jane, her husband, and Northumberland were imprisoned, found guilty of **treason**, and condemned to death.

Edward founded Christ's Hospital School, known as the Bluecoat School.

Lady Jane Grey. Her father and the Duke of Northumberland plotted to make her queen. The 15-year old Jane fainted when told she was queen, four days after Edward's death.

MARY I (Bloody Mary)
1553-1558 (b. 1516)

Thomas Cranmer, the first Protestant Archbishop of Canterbury, is burned at the stake in 1556.

MARY I

Mary's first acts as queen were to have the scheming Northumberland executed, and then to re-establish the Catholic Church; for Mary was a Catholic like her mother, Catherine of Aragon.

At first, Mary behaved fairly towards convinced Protestants, letting them leave the country. But in 1554 Sir Thomas Wyatt led a rebellion in protest against Mary's planned marriage to Philip, Catholic heir to the throne of Spain. Lady Jane Grey's father was among the rebels. Mary executed over 100 people, including the innocent Lady Jane and her husband. She even suspected her own sister Elizabeth and imprisoned her. Mary then married Philip. After a year she had not become pregnant, and Philip left to

rule Spain. The unhappy Mary tried to convert the whole kingdom to Catholicism. She **persecuted** Protestants, and burned many at the stake. This earned her the nickname 'Bloody Mary'. Protestant feeling in England was strengthened.

In 1557 Mary and Philip went to war against France, and in 1558 the French won Calais, the last of England's possessions in France. Mary died brokenhearted, for English rule in France was dear to her.

Road works in Mary's reign. She reformed the country's financial affairs and improved its roads.

English whaling boat. In 1557 English whale fishing started at Spitzbergen, Norway.

ELIZABETH I
1558-1603 (b. 1533)

ELIZABETH I

Elizabeth I was a wise and careful **monarch**. She showed this by choosing excellent advisers, Sir William Cecil, better known as Lord Burghley and, later, his son Robert Cecil. She restored the Protestant religion, closing down the refounded Catholic monasteries, and made herself supreme head of a single English church, as her father Henry VIII had been. Her Catholic cousin, Mary, the Scottish queen, became a threat to her. When Mary's husband Francis became king of France, Mary called herself 'Queen of England and Scotland'. King Francis died in 1560, and Mary returned to Scotland. She was soon **deposed** and imprisoned, since she was suspected of helping in the murder of her second husband, Lord Darnley.

The execution of Mary, Queen of Scots. Mary had been Elizabeth's captive for nineteen years. Elizabeth did not want her executed, although Mary had plotted against her; but she had to give the order. Elizabeth was furious that her order to kill Mary had been carried out, however, and punished the official who had sent the order through.

Mary escaped, and asked for Elizabeth's help. Elizabeth kept her semi-captive. But Mary remained the focus of Catholic plotting. In 1586 Mary was found to have joined in a plot, led by Anthony Babington, to kill Elizabeth. Reluctantly, Elizabeth had Mary executed. Mary met her death with great courage, even when the first blow of the axe failed to go through her neck, and she whispered, 'Sweet Jesus'.

Elizabeth never married, although early in her reign it seemed that she might wed her favourite, Robert Dudley, after the sudden and mysterious death of his wife. Dudley stayed her favourite until his death in 1588.

William Shakespeare (1564-1616), England's greatest dramatist. His plays were performed in the Globe Theatre, London.

In the 1560s, English merchant seamen began to capture African people and sell them as slaves.

ELIZABETH I
1558-1603 (b. 1533)

In 1579, just after Dudley's second marriage, Elizabeth came close to marrying the French Duke of Alençon. The English disliked the idea of foreign interference, and still fiercely opposed the Catholic religion (which Alençon followed); so Elizabeth gave up the idea of marriage. She had other favourites, including Sir Walter Raleigh and the Earl of Essex. She became known as 'The Virgin Queen', and Sir Walter Raleigh named the American state of Virginia after her, when he claimed it for England.

Elizabeth's reign saw a flowering of the arts, invention, and exploration. Her court welcomed English musicians, painters and poets. The period also saw the emergence of some of the greatest English writers, such as William Shakespeare and Christopher Marlowe. The first flush lavatory was invented, and some London houses had water pumped from a central supply. In 1581

Sir Walter Raleigh brought tobacco and potatoes to England from America.

the explorer Francis Drake was knighted, after completing the first English round-the-world voyage. Later Sir Walter Raleigh set off in search of **El Dorado**.

In 1588, angered by Elizabeth's treatment of Catholics, by Mary Queen of Scots' execution, and by English interference in a war between Spain and Holland, King Philip of Spain sent a war fleet, the Armada, to attack England. The weather was against the Spanish, and the English, commanded by Sir Francis Drake, easily defeated them off the coast of France; a second Armada, six years later, was scattered by storms.

Elizabeth managed money very well; she gradually paid all England's debts, and was able to reduce taxes in the 1570s. War was expensive, though, and the Spanish war sent the treasury back into debt; it remained in debt at Elizabeth's death, though the amount was not great.

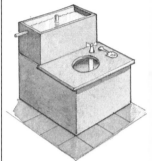

The first flush lavatory, built about 1595 near Bath by Sir John Harrington, Elizabeth's godson. Elizabeth is said to have ordered one. It had a sloping bowl made of lead or stone and a wooden seat, and a clamp to stop people flushing it just for fun.

Sir Francis Drake and the Spanish Armada.

JAMES I
1603-1625 (b. 1566)

JAMES I

James, son of Mary, Queen of Scots, was already king of Scotland; he was a witty and wise speaker. The English people were tired of Elizabeth, who could be fussy and a ditherer, and welcomed him gladly. James behaved harshly to Catholics and to a group of extreme Protestants, the **Puritans**, and several Catholic plots against him were exposed. The most famous was the Gunpowder Plot, discovered in 1605 when Guy Fawkes and other Catholics were found in the cellars of

The Mayflower *and a 'Pilgrim Father'.*

The 'Authorised Version' of the Bible. In 1611 James authorised a translation of the Bible from Latin into English. This translation is still in use today.

the **House of Commons** preparing to blow up King James and Parliament.

These plots increased public sympathy for James, but not for long. His deeds were not as wise as his words. He believed in the **Divine Right of Kings**, and so thought he had God's authority. He argued with

Parliament over everything. In 1614 the Parliament of that year was called 'The Addled Parliament' because they could not agree on anything, so that no Acts could be passed. After this James ruled without Parliament.

He continued to persecute Puritans, and in 1620 a group of them, later known as the 'Pilgrim Fathers', sailed to America in the *Mayflower* to escape him. They founded a settlement in Pennsylvania.

Then in 1621 James had to recall Parliament because he needed money to help his son-in-law, the Dutch king, to repel a Spanish invasion.

James became very unpopular. He seemed weak and foolish, and was devoted to his favourite, the Duke of Buckingham. He was also very fond of alcoholic drink.

Guy Fawkes is caught preparing to blow up the Houses of Parliament in 1605.

Sir Walter Raleigh. James imprisoned him for treason. In 1616 he released him to look for El Dorado. (James needed money.) In 1618 Raleigh returned empty-handed and James had him executed.

CHARLES I

CHARLES I
1625-1649 (b. 1600)

Charles inherited a mess from his father, and he repeated many of James's mistakes. Like his father, he believed that he ruled by God's command. In 1629 he too dissolved Parliament, and ruled without it until 1640. He raised money by forcing loans from the wealthy, selling knighthoods, and with many unfair and unpopular taxes. He took more notice of his father's favourite, the Duke of Buckingham, than of wise advisers. Buckingham's pride and temper led Charles into costly wars with France and Spain. But in 1628 Buckingham was murdered, and Charles began to follow the advice of his queen, Henrietta Maria. This did not please Protestants, for the queen was a Catholic. In 1638 a group of Scottish Protestants made a solemn vow (called the '**Covenant**') to defend their religion against Charles's attempts to change it, and in 1640 they invaded England. Charles fell out with his new Parliament, and dismissed it.

The first use of wallpaper, as a cheap alternative to tapestry, was in about 1645.

In 1642, Charles took soldiers to the House of Commons to arrest five members of the House for plotting with the Covenanters. But they had been warned and had fled, and the people of London hid them. Charles realised that Parliament was against him, and left London. He gathered his supporters, known as the Royalists, and declared war on Parliament. During this war, the Civil War, Oliver Cromwell emerged as a fine general and in 1644 trained the '**New Model Army**'. It defeated the Royalist forces, and in 1646 Charles surrendered in Scotland and was handed over to his enemies. In January 1649 Charles was tried and executed.

Bananas were on sale in shops in Britain for the first time in 1633.

Charles's execution: he wore two shirts, so that he would not shiver with cold and seem frightened; he also asked the executioner not to cut off his beard, as it had 'caused no offence'. His calm dignity moved and impressed everyone who saw or heard of it.

CHARLES II
1660-1685 (b. 1630)

Charles's heir, also named Charles, took the oath of the Covenant in 1650 in Scotland, where he was proclaimed king by the Scots. He gathered supporters and in 1651 joined battle with the **Parliamentarians**. Charles was defeated at the Battle of Worcester, and he fled to join his mother in France.

In 1653 Oliver Cromwell made himself head of state, and became as tyrannical as any king. He was a strict Puritan, and banned entertainment and the wearing of bright colours. In 1655 he dissolved Parliament and ruled the country with the army. In 1658 he died; his son Richard took his place, but he **abdicated** in 1659. General Monk, a soldier who wanted the king back, took over, gathered loyal Royalists, and asked Charles II to return. Charles declared that he would pardon everyone except those directly

Many English pubs are called the 'Royal Oak'. They are named after the great oak tree in which Charles II hid after his defeat at the Battle of Worcester.

ROYAL OAK

involved in his father's death. In 1660 he returned and the monarchy was restored.

The new king was welcomed rapturously by huge crowds, tired of Cromwell's harsh rule. Charles was called 'the Merrie Monarch', and he cancelled all Cromwell's Acts; in May 1661 a 40-metre-high (130 feet) maypole was erected and people danced happily. But Charles had known great sadness, and his love of pleasure was balanced by caution. He was determined not to lose the throne, nor to plunge England again into such hardship. He kept quiet about his belief in the Divine Right of Kings, and his Catholic sympathies; for the majority of the people were determined to keep Catholics off the English throne. Unfortunately Charles's wife, the Portuguese Catherine of Braganza, bore no children. Charles had fourteen children by his mistresses, but **illegitimate** children could not inherit the throne. The next heir was his Catholic brother James!

OLIVER CROMWELL
1649-1658

Oliver Cromwell. The English hated his strict rule, which outlawed pleasure.

The Great Fire of London, 1666. It helped to purify the city after the terrible outbreak of bubonic plague in 1665. It destroyed about 13,000 houses in four days. Charles helped to clean up.

JAMES II
1685-1688 (b. 1633)

Soon after Charles II's death the Duke of Monmouth, Charles's eldest illegitimate son, was proclaimed king by a group of Protestant rebels. James II, Charles II's brother, defeated the rebels at the Battle of Sedgemoor. Monmouth was executed.

James was wilful and tactless, and believed strongly in the Divine Right of Kings. He dismissed Parliament and cancelled many of the anti-Catholic laws, and persecuted Protestants. People were discontented; but they did not want another civil war. So they pinned their hopes on James's heir, his daughter Mary. She was a Protestant, and wife of the Protestant King William of Orange (now part of the Netherlands). In 1688, however, James's second wife, the

The Battle of Sedgemoor, 6 July 1685. James's army completely crushed the Duke of Monmouth's rebellion.

Judge Jeffreys (known as 'the hanging judge') conducts the 'Bloody Assizes'. This was the trial of Monmouth's supporters after the Battle of Sedgemoor. They were shown no mercy – 320 were executed and over 800 condemned to slavery.

Catholic Mary of Modena (in Spain), had a son. This horrified the English who had not forgotten 'Bloody Mary' (Mary I). They would not accept a line of Catholic rulers, since the Protestant religion was at last securely established. So Parliament invited William of Orange and Mary to rule England. James's men deserted him, and he fled to France.

Isaac Newton. Watching a falling apple prompted him to work out the laws of gravity in 1665. His theory of gravity was published in 1685, and his great work on physics, the Principia, in 1687.

WILLIAM
1689-1702 (b. 1650) and
MARY
1689-1694 (b. 1662)

James Edward Stuart (1688-1766), admired for his intelligence and his good looks. He was brought up at the French court, where in 1701 he was proclaimed King of England and Scotland. But he never ruled.

Mary was James II's daughter, but her baby half-brother was the rightful heir. William was also descended from Charles I, but even further removed from the royal line of descent. Again Parliament had stepped in to stop a king who believed that he had the right to do whatever he liked. Still, James was fortunate; Charles I had lost his life for crossing Parliament.

Mary refused to rule without William. William, on his side, insisted that he should be king, and not just **Regent**. Parliament had

The Bank of England, founded in 1694 to do the government's financial business.

to accept this. Even so, it was clear that Parliament was now more powerful than the monarch. They proceeded to make certain of this by issuing two **Declarations**: monarchs would not be allowed either to make or cancel laws, or to have an army, without

Parliament's consent; and Parliament had to be summoned to meet regularly.

In 1690 James, with Irish support, tried to regain his crown. William's forces defeated him at the Battle of the Boyne. Mary took little part in politics. She was a devoted wife, and William was heartbroken when she died of smallpox in 1694.

The Catholic countries of Europe did not like England's Protestantism, nor did they like the loss of royal power and the breaking of the laws of succession, for it set a dangerous example. The Catholic Church and its European monarchs wanted to hold on to their power. France made war on England, trying to restore James as king. When James died in 1701, King Louis XIV of France called James's son, James Edward, 'King of Great Britain and Ireland'. Meanwhile, William's lack of charm and his increasing brutality towards Catholics made him unpopular in England. He was not much mourned after his death in a riding accident.

The Massacre of Glencoe. The Scots supported the exiled James II. William made them swear loyalty to him and Mary. The MacDonalds of Glencoe took the oath a few days late. In revenge, William asked their ancient enemies, the Campbells, to kill them all. The Campbells accepted the MacDonalds' hospitality, then, on 13 February 1692, they murdered thirty-eight MacDonalds. After the Scots realised William had ordered this, they never trusted him again.

ANNE
1702-1714 (b. 1665)

Defoe wrote Robinson Crusoe, based on the real adventures of the Scottish sailor Alexander Selkirk, rescued that year from a desert island where he had lived for four years.

ANNE

Anne took more interest in drinking tea (a new fashion) and betting on horse races than in affairs of state. John Churchill, the husband of Anne's favourite, Sarah, became one of the finest and most renowned of English generals. Under him, the British army and its allies kept Spain from taking over most of Europe, and ended France's support of the Stuart claim to the English throne.

Even so, Anne's life was troubled because of problems connected with the succession. She had joined other Protestants in offering the throne to William and Mary, but she never forgave herself for betraying her father, James II. She believed that her ill health, and the loss of seventeen children either during pregnancy or in their early childhood, was a punishment. As she was left childless, another heir had to be chosen. This was very

difficult. James's Catholic son and grandson would never be allowed to reign, but Anne and her advisers did not like the alternative. This was the ruling house of Hanover in Germany. Its members were descended from Charles I's sister Elizabeth, who had married the King of Bohemia.

A German monarch would not be welcome. On the other hand, James II's son, James Edward Stuart, would not give up his Catholic faith. There were no more surviving descendants of Charles I himself, so the Hanoverians were invited to take the throne.

Blenheim Palace and the Duke of Marlborough. In gratitude for his brilliant military leadership, Anne gave John Churchill the title Duke of Marlborough. The great architect Vanbrugh designed Blenheim Palace in Oxfordshire for the Duke, to commemorate his first great victory, at the Battle of Blenheim in 1704.

Queen Anne loved watching the horses at the races.

GEORGE I
1714-1727 (b. 1660)

Weaving tools and machinery. Improvements in these during George's reign increased production. This was the start of the 'Industrial Revolution' which transformed British life in the 18th and 19th centuries.

GEORGE I

At Anne's death the crown went to George, Elector (ruler) of Hanover in Germany. Georg did not like England, and he knew that the English did not really want him as their king, but had chosen his family just to keep the Catholic Stuarts out. He preferred Hanover, his home, where he had absolute power.

George hated painting and poetry. He did enjoy music, and brought the great composer Handel to England. But George rarely visited England and never learnt English. In 1721

one of the government **ministers** was given the job of speaking for the king in meetings. This man, Robert Walpole, was called the 'prime' (meaning 'chief') minister.

Because George had so little interest in governing England, the **monarchy** had even less power by the end of his reign. His eldest son was also called George; the two hated each other, for the son had never forgiven his father for divorcing his mother.

GEORGE II

As king, George II resembled George I, the father he had hated so much. He even hated *his* eldest son, Frederick. British military success continued. In 1743 George himself led his troops to victory against France at the Battle of Dettingen. During the Seven Years War (1756-63), when Britain and Prussia (part of what is now Germany) fought France to gain **colonies** in India and America, William Pitt became a great military leader. By 1759 Britain ruled the seas, and owned most of Canada, India, and the West Indies.

When Frederick died in 1751, his son, another George, became George II's successor.

GEORGE II
1727-1760 (b. 1683)

'Bonnie Prince Charlie' (Charles, son of James Edward Stuart), the 'Young Pretender', escapes after the failure of his attempt in 1745 to gain the throne. This was the second 'Jacobite rebellion'.

1752 SEPTEMBER
1 2 (14) 15 16 1
18 19 20 21 22 23
25 26 27

In 1752 the Gregorian calendar was adopted. It was twelve days ahead of the old (Julian) calendar, so the day after 2 September was called 14 September. People rioted, believing their lives had been shortened.

GEORGE III

GEORGE III
1760-1820 (b. 1738)

George III was the first Hanoverian king to be born in Britain; he was known as 'Farmer George' because of his interest in agriculture. He regained some of the power lost by George I, but he did not keep it.

Britain was now a very powerful nation, owning many colonies – but guarding them was costly. The American colonists protested at the heavy taxes that Britain made them pay, and in 1770 all American taxes were abolished except the tax on tea. This one tax was kept so that Britain would not lose the right to tax Americans. Boston, in Massachusetts, rebelled against the tea tax. Britain took away Boston's rights as a colony. This angered all Americans, and in 1775 the War of Independence (now called the American Revolution) began between Britain and America. France and Holland supported the colonists, and in 1783,

The Boston Tea Party. In 1770 British troops shot dead five anti-tax protesters in Boston, Massachusetts. In 1773 a group of angry Bostonians dressed up as American Indians and tipped British tea cargoes into the sea.

after Britain's surrender, American independence was officially recognised.

Britain was more successful in the other great conflict of George's reign. Two great leaders, Lord Horatio Nelson at sea, and the Duke of Wellington on land, defeated Napoleon, **dictatorial** Emperor of the newly formed French **Republic**, in **campaigns** conducted between 1793 and 1815.

At home, the Industrial Revolution was at its peak, and Britain's wealth increased. A group called the Luddites rioted, and smashed machinery, fearing that it would take jobs away from working people. They were proved right in 1816. After the expense of the war in Europe, other countries could no longer afford to buy British goods. Jobs were lost, and poverty ruled.

By this time George no longer held power. He had shown signs of madness in 1788. By 1810 he was quite mad and his son, George, was Prince Regent, acting for the king.

The Battle of Waterloo, 18 June 1815. The British and Prussian armies under Wellington and General Blücher overcame Napoleon's French forces.

Lord Nelson, at the Battle of Copenhagen 1801, puts his telescope to his blind eye, so as to ignore a command to retreat.

GEORGE IV
1820–1830 (b. 1762)

Brighton Pavilion, designed for George by the architect John Nash. Nash's buildings can also be seen in Bath, and Regent's Park, London. Their style is imitated today.

GEORGE IV

George IV had been a stylish Prince of Wales, but his wild behaviour brought disgrace to the monarchy. The country was poor, after the expense of the wars against Napoleon, and unemployment was high. George was soon hated for his lavish spending, and for treating his wife, whom he disliked, very badly. He had been forced to marry her, and he did not find her at all attractive. He tried to divorce her, but she died in 1821, which saved him the trouble. George was so pigheaded and selfish that the **Whigs**, who were not then in power, agreed that when they had the chance they would remove all remaining royal power.

George's one good point was that he loved and encouraged the arts and architecture. The beautiful 'Regency' style of architecture was named after him, because it emerged with George's encouragement when he was Prince Regent (1811–20).

William IV, George's younger brother, was known as 'the Sailor King', because he had been a sailor from the age of thirteen. He hated ceremony, and his sensible behaviour was a refreshing change. He tried to hold on to what little power the **sovereign** still had, and opposed the Reform **Bills** of 1831 and 1832, which aimed to take away that power. When rioting followed the blocking of the Third Reform Bill, William gave in, losing the last remnants of power.

WILLIAM IV
1830-1837 (b. 1765)

*Tolpuddle martyrs. In 1834 a group of farm labourers, known as the Tolpuddle martyrs, were transported to Australia for forming a **trade union**.*

The movement towards greater security for workers grew. Trade unions were established to stand up for workers' rights. The Chartist Movement demanded votes for all men. Slavery was abolished in British colonies. Now workers had to be paid to do the work the slaves had been forced to do. The new Poor Law of 1834 provided 'workhouses' to give shelter to the penniless. For them, with no **Welfare State**, unemployment could mean starvation.

A horse-drawn London bus.

VICTORIA
1837-1901 (b. 1819)

In 1854 Britain and France took Turkey's side in a war against Russia; this became known as the Crimean War (it was fought in the Russian territory called the Crimea). Other European countries later entered the war on the British side. British forces suffered severely from lack of planning; and in the disastrous 'Charge of the Light Brigade', a mistaken order sent almost 700 men of the Light Brigade into a narrow valley, facing a battery of Russian guns. A third of them were killed.

VICTORIA

After William IV's death the crown passed to his young niece, Victoria. The new queen was only eighteen and had led a sheltered life. At her **accession**, Hanover and Britain ceased to be ruled together, because the laws of succession in Hanover barred a woman from ruling.

Victoria had a natural authority, but she quickly became dependent on the prime minister, Lord Melbourne, adopting all his opinions. As his attitudes were old-fashioned and strict, Victoria quickly became very unpopular.

In 1840 she married her cousin, Prince Albert of Saxe-Coburg-Gotha (in Germany), and things changed. Albert was not outgoing, and was never much liked

by the British people. But Victoria adored him, and Albert's influence on her, and so on British life, was enormous. Fortunately, Albert was kindhearted, peace-loving, and in many ways open-minded. Family values and strict morality were very important. Albert was given the title 'Prince **Consort**' in 1857, but died of typhoid four years later. On his deathbed he wrote a letter to the president of America, Abraham Lincoln, in connection with a crisis that had flared up between Britain and America. The careful wording of the letter prevented the outbreak of war between the two countries. At the same time, Albert was also worried about reports that his son Edward, Prince of Wales, had been conducting a very public love-affair with an actress in Ireland.

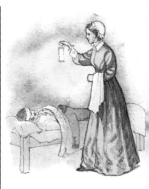

Florence Nightingale, 'the Lady with the Lamp', became famous for the quality of nursing care she provided in the Crimea. She and her team of nurses brought the death rate for injured soldiers down from 42% to 2%.

Prince Albert had the Crystal Palace built to house his brainchild, the Great Exhibition of 1851. The Crystal Palace was designed by Joseph Paxton and made of glass on an iron frame.

VICTORIA
1837-1901 (b. 1819)

Disraeli (right) and Gladstone (left) in the House of Commons. Disraeli was a Conservative. Gladstone, whom Victoria disliked, was a Liberal. They were fierce opponents and held office as prime minister alternately in Victoria's reign.

Victoria was devastated by her husband Albert's death. She blamed their son Edward for causing it by his wild behaviour, and never forgave him. She wore black, in mourning, for the rest of her life, and made no public appearances for over twenty years.

Her popularity crashed, and there was even talk of abolishing the monarchy, but in 1887 she returned to public life, and her Diamond **Jubilee** in 1897 was a time of great celebration. Since Albert's death Victoria had relied mainly on a Scottish servant, John Brown. She remained very close to him, despite public disapproval. She also very much liked Benjamin Disraeli, prime minister from 1874 to 1880. Disraeli made her Empress of India in 1876, and she was grief-stricken at his death in 1881.

Victoria's reign was coloured by her strong feelings, and most of all, her deep grief at the

= *The British Empire in 1899.*

loss of Albert. She was strong-willed, as well, and her personality and beliefs affected national life. She believed in strict morality. She really cared about working people, believing that they were the heart of Britain. Her reign saw the limiting of the working day to ten hours, the introduction of basic education for all, and other measures aimed at improving the conditions of the poor.

Victoria lived so long, and had had so many children, that she was eventually a senior figure in all the royal families of Europe. This brought her considerable influence and authority. She was even called 'the grandmother of Europe'. This was one of the reasons why, after the Crimean War, her reign saw a long period of peace in Europe.

By the time Victoria died in 1901, Britain was the most powerful nation in the world, at the head of a vast empire, and with influence in the rest of Europe.

British settlers riding on an Indian elephant. British territory in India had been growing since 1600.

EDWARD VII

EDWARD VII
1901-1910 (b. 1841)

Edward laughed so much at a Royal Command Performance of a play by George Bernard Shaw that he broke his chair.

Victoria's son Edward had been very strictly brought up, and both his parents had disliked him. In spite of all this, he was a kind man, although he had the hot temper of the Hanoverians. He was popular, for he was deeply concerned about the conditions of the poor, and the gap between rich and poor.

Society was changing rapidly. In 1906

Emmeline Pankhurst started the **Suffragette Movement**, demanding that women be given the right to vote in parliamentary elections. Edward earned the title 'the Peacemaker' because of his efforts to bring about good relations with other countries. He also foresaw the possibility that Germany, a nation greedy for power, might cause a major war. His death occurred in the middle of a crisis, after the **House of Lords** rejected a Liberal budget aimed at helping the poor.

The first Boy Scout camp took place on Brownsea Island, Dorset, in 1907.

GEORGE V

Edward's son, George V, was a sailor like William IV. He was shy, and he disliked ceremony. He took his duties very seriously. In 1917 he gave up his family name of Saxe-Coburg-Gotha and took the surname 'Windsor', after Windsor Castle. He did this because his original name was German, and Britain and Germany were at war.

In the 1930s most of the population became poverty-stricken in the economic crisis known as the 'Great Depression'. George was very concerned and went to meet

GEORGE V
1910-1936 (b. 1865)

In 1913 suffragette Emily Davidson threw herself in front of George's horse in the Derby.

people who were suffering hardship. He also gave up part of his own income.

In 1935 George was genuinely surprised at the extent of the celebrations of his Silver Jubilee. He had not realised he was so popular, and that people liked him. He died peacefully the following year. He was one of the very few monarchs in Europe who had kept his throne after the First World War.

*In 1919 the **Irish Republican Army** (IRA) was founded to free Ireland from British rule.*

GEORGE VI
1936-1952 (b. 1895)

GEORGE VI

George V's eldest son, Edward, was a popular Prince of Wales. He was charming and handsome, and cared about poor people. He was brave, too, and had wanted to fight in the First World War.

Unfortunately, at the time of George's death, Edward was in love with a married woman, the American Mrs Simpson. In October 1936 she and her husband divorced, and Edward seemed set on marrying her. This was impossible, as he was now head of the Church of England, and the Church did not approve of divorce. This royal marriage drama overshadowed important issues such as unemployment, the civil war in Spain, and the rise to power, in Germany, of Adolf Hitler. In December 1936, Edward abdicated, and his brother, the Duke of York, became George VI.

EDWARD VIII
Jan-Dec 1936 (b. 1894)

Edward and his wife-to-be, Wallis Simpson. After their marriage they were known as the Duke and Duchess of Windsor.

George VI was a shy, frail man, with a stammer. He found kingship difficult. His wife, Elizabeth, was his biggest asset. During the Second World War (1939-45) Adolf Hitler, the German leader, called her 'the most dangerous woman in Europe'. This was because her courage and cheerfulness inspired and comforted the whole nation. When bombing started, she was asked to take her two daughters to safety in Canada. She refused. Even when Buckingham Palace was bombed, she remained cheerful, saying, 'Now I can look the East End in the face.' (The East End of London had been bombed shortly before.) The couple, and their daughters, Elizabeth and Margaret, presented a picture of contented and dutiful family life, giving a sense of security to a nation at war.

Gandhi led the peaceful movement for Indian independence. In 1947 years of struggle in India ended with independence for India and Pakistan. During George's reign many other colonies became independent, with Britain's encouragement. Britain's power was seen as more of a moral influence on some of the newly independent nations.

George and Elizabeth visited London's East End after it was bombed during the Second World War.

ELIZABETH II
1952- (b. 1926)

During Elizabeth's reign, everyday life has changed in many ways. She has shown a sense of duty, common sense and concern for her subjects, including those of the British **Commonwealth**. She and her husband, the Duke of Edinburgh, have made efforts to 'modernise' the image of the royal family. They have talked about their lives on television. Her children were sent off to school, not taught privately at home. She has also been an **ambassador** of goodwill for Britain worldwide. She has virtually no political power, but she takes her job seriously. She has seen many prime ministers come and go – her experience and common sense could be valuable to any prime minister who cares to use them.

Elizabeth is a strong-minded woman; she has taken great care with her public image. In 1953, when she was crowned, television was still a novelty. Elizabeth insisted, against the advice of Prime Minister Winston Churchill and the Archbishop of Canterbury, that her coronation ceremony must be televised.

Charles, Prince of Wales, and his wife Diana kiss on the balcony of Buckingham Palace, on their wedding day in 1981. Their stormy marriage ended in separation in December 1992.

Attitudes to women, and therefore to marriage, have changed enormously since World War II, and the 1960s saw a revolution in sexual morality. Marriage today is a partnership; 100 years ago the husband 'owned' his wife. Changes like this take time, and there is some confusion in society about the nature of marriage now; divorce has become very common. The royal family is no exception. In 1955 Princess Margaret, Elizabeth's sister, gave up the man she loved because he had been divorced. In the 1990s all three of the queen's married children have separated from their partners. The marriage problems of Charles, Prince of Wales, and his wife Diana made headlines for years.

The monarchy has become less popular, and in 1992 the Queen chose to pay taxes, as well as finding other ways of cutting the cost of the royal family, including opening Buckingham Palace to the public.

Elizabeth's reign has not been easy, but she is always dignified and discreet.

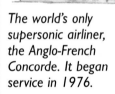

The world's only supersonic airliner, the Anglo-French Concorde. It began service in 1976.

*In 1971 Britain began using the **decimal** system of coinage.*

GLOSSARY

abdicate to give up being monarch

accession a monarch's coming to the throne

ambassador someone who represents his or her country abroad

aristocracy the people of the highest rank or class

Bill a proposed law which has not yet been approved by the monarch or by Parliament

campaign a series of military actions aimed at a particular result

colony a territory taken and governed by one country, located in another country; a colonist is a settler there

Commonwealth the group of nations which were once ruled by Britain, and now govern themselves

consort the husband or wife of a monarch

Covenant an agreement made in 1638 by a group of Scots, to protect their special form of Protestant worship. It was entered into in 1643 by English Parliamentarians

decimal a counting system based on the number ten

Declaration an official announcement

depose to force a monarch from the throne

dictatorial exercising power selfishly and cruelly

Divine Right of Kings the belief that a monarch by birth rules by God's will rather than by the people's will

El Dorado (means 'the golden' in Spanish) a mythical country full of gold

feudal system the division of society into classes. Each class worked for the class above in exchange for land and protection

heir the person, usually the monarch's eldest son, who has the right to inherit wealth and rank

House of Commons the British House of Parliament whose members are chosen by vote, and have most of the power in government

House of Lords the British House of Parliament whose members are peers and bishops, with little power

illegitimate born to parents who were not legally married

invalid not legally acceptable

Irish Republican Army (IRA) a group set up in 1919 to fight for Irish independence from Britain, and union between Northern and Southern Ireland

Jubilee an anniversary, especially of a monarch's coronation

minister a person whose job is to take part in government

monarch a king or queen

monarchy government under a king or queen

New Model Army the well-trained army created in 1645 by Oliver Cromwell during the English Civil War

Parliamentarians the people who supported Parliament against the king in the English Civil War

persecute abuse and mistreat someone, especially because of his or her nationality or religion

Puritans a group who wanted to go further than most Protestants in the measures they took to rid the Church of immoral elements

Regent someone appointed to rule for a monarch who is too young, or ill, or absent

Renaissance the flowering of art and learning which took place, starting in Italy, during the 14th to 17th centuries

Republic a self-governing country ruled by an elected president, not a monarch

sovereign a monarch

Suffragette Movement a campaign in the early 20th century fighting for women's right to vote

trade union an organised group of workers in a particular trade, formed to protect the rights of all workers in that trade

treason the crime of betraying the monarch or the nation

Wars of the Roses the name given in the 19th century to the thirty-year (1455-85) struggle for the crown between the houses of Lancaster and York

Welfare State the system established in the 1940s to protect the poor, providing housing, an income, and health care

Whigs the British political party in the 17th to 19th centuries that opposed the monarchy

INDEX

Kings *and* Queens
— *of England* —

ABOUT FAMILY TREES

This family tree shows the family relationships between English monarchs.

The dates under each monarch's name indicate when he or she reigned. By looking at these dates, you can see the order in which the monarchs ruled.

In family trees the eldest child is always shown on the left and the youngest on the right. The eldest son normally rules first.

Different coloured lines denote different families or royal houses.

Edward III

John of Gaunt
Duke of Lancaster

John Beaufort
Marquess of Somerset

THE TUDOR CLAIM TO THE THRONE

John Beaufort
Duke of Somerset

Margaret Beaufort

Katherine of France
married Owen Tudor

Edmund Tudor *married*
Earl of Richmond

Katherine of France was Henry V's queen. After Henry's death, she married Owen Tudor. Their descendants formed the Tudor royal house.

THE TUDORS

Henry VII

1536 | *Start of dissolution of monasteries*